Let's Celebrate Freedom!

THE WOMEN'S SUFFRAGE MOVEMENT

Lorijo Metz

PowerKiDS
press

New York

Dedicated to my mother, Barbara Rush, who always encouraged me to be more!

Published in 2014 by The Rosen Publishing Group, Inc.
29 East 21st Street, New York, NY 10010

First Edition

Editor: Amelie von Zumbusch
Book Design: Colleen Bialecki
Photo Research: Katie Stryker

Photo Credits: Cover, p. 7 Stock Montage/Contributor/Archive Photos/Getty Images; p. 4 Hill Street Studios/Blend Images/Getty Images; p. 5 Time & Life Pictures/Contributor/Getty Images; p. 6 MPI/Stringer/Archive Photos/Getty Images; p. 8 Dennis Macdonald/Photolibrary/Getty Images; pp. 9, 13 (top) Library of Congress Prints and Photographs Division Washington, D.C., p. 10 Jeffrey M. Frank/Shutterstock.com; p. 12 Thomas Waterman Wood/The Bridgeman Art Library/Getty Images; pp. 13 (bottom), 19 Underwood Archives/Contributor/Archive Photos/Getty Images; pp. 14, 15 Portrait of Susan B. Anthony and Elizabeth Cady Stanton by Robert Shetterly. © Robert Shetterly / Americans Who Tell the Truth; p. 17 FPG/Staff/Archive Photos/Getty Images; p. 20 Steve Northup/Contributor/TIME & LIFE Images/Getty Images; p. 21 auremar/Shutterstock.com; p. 22 Hill Street Studios/Blend Images/Getty Images.

Library of Congress Cataloging-in-Publication Data

Metz, Lorijo.
The women's suffrage movement / by Lorijo Metz. — First edition.
    pages cm. — (Let's celebrate freedom)
Includes index.
ISBN 978-1-4777-2898-7 (library) — ISBN 978-1-4777-2987-8 (pbk.) —
ISBN 978-1-4777-3057-7 (6-pack)
1. Women—Suffrage—United States—History—Juvenile literature. I. Title.
JK1896M47 2013
324.6'230973—dc23

2013022502

Manufactured in the United States of America

CPSIA Compliance Information: Batch # W14PK4: For Further Information contact Rosen Publishing, New York, New York at 1-800-237-9932

CONTENTS

In 1840, Americans Elizabeth Cady Stanton and Lucretia Mott met at the World Anti-Slavery **Convention** in London. Both strongly believed that slavery was wrong. Both wanted to share their ideas on **abolishing**, or ending, it. Both were barred from taking part in the convention because they were women.

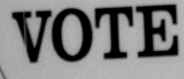

Today, the right to vote gives American women a voice in government.

Lucretia Mott was born in Nantucket, Massachusetts, in 1793. She later moved to Philadelphia, Pennsylvania. She belonged to the Quaker faith and became a minister in 1821.

Something important happened that day. Stanton and Mott began talking about holding their own convention. They believed that women deserved the same rights as men. It was time to fight for women's **suffrage**, or the right to vote. Eight years later, they held America's first women's rights convention in Seneca Falls, New York.

In the past, American women had fewer rights. Women in the 1700s could not own land or vote. They were expected to marry, have large families, and live by their husbands' rules. Wives raised and cared for their children, but their husbands always had the final say.

In addition to cooking and cleaning, women made everyday items like butter, clothing, and soap.

Between 1775 and 1783, Americans fought the **American Revolution** to break free of British rule. Since the men were off fighting, women did many of their jobs. Along with their own work, women hunted for food and managed farms and businesses. After the war, many women wondered why they couldn't have the same rights as men.

Abigail Adams argued that the leaders of the American Revolution should "remember the ladies" and "not put such unlimited power into the hands of the husbands."

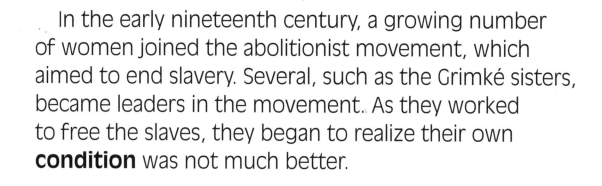

In the early nineteenth century, a growing number of women joined the abolitionist movement, which aimed to end slavery. Several, such as the Grimké sisters, became leaders in the movement. As they worked to free the slaves, they began to realize their own **condition** was not much better.

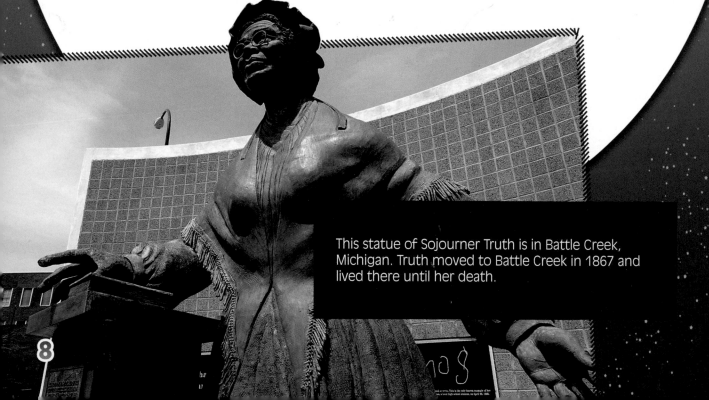

This statue of Sojourner Truth is in Battle Creek, Michigan. Truth moved to Battle Creek in 1867 and lived there until her death.

Sarah Grimké (left) and Angelina Grimké Weld (right) were sisters from Charleston, South Carolina. They were among the first women to give antislavery speeches.

Abolitionists, such as Lucretia Mott and Susan B. Anthony, became early leaders in the fight for women's rights. Former slave Sojourner Truth was another early leader. In 1854, she gave her famous "Ain't I a Woman?" speech in Akron, Ohio. It helped others understand her sufferings as both a slave and a woman.

In 1848, Stanton and Mott organized a convention in Seneca Falls, New York, to talk about women's rights. More than 300 people, including 40 men, attended. Former slave and famous abolitionist Frederick Douglass spoke in support of women's rights.

Stanton and Mott created a list of rights they believed women should have, called the Declaration of Sentiments. They modeled it on the **Declaration of Independence**, in which the Americans listed their reasons for breaking away from British rule. The Declaration of Sentiments said women deserved the right to vote. It also argued they should have other rights, such as the rights to a career and education.

This is Elizabeth Cady Stanton's home in Seneca Falls, New York. Today it is part of a national historical park.

TIMELINE

June 20, 1840

Elizabeth Cady Stanton and Lucretia Mott meet at the World Anti-Slavery Convention.

July 19–20, 1848

The first women's rights convention takes place in Seneca Falls, New York.

1840 1850 1860 1870 1880 1890 1900

December 10, 1869

Lawmakers in Wyoming Territory sign a law giving women the right to vote.

March 30, 1870

The Fifteenth **Amendment** grants African-American men the right to vote.

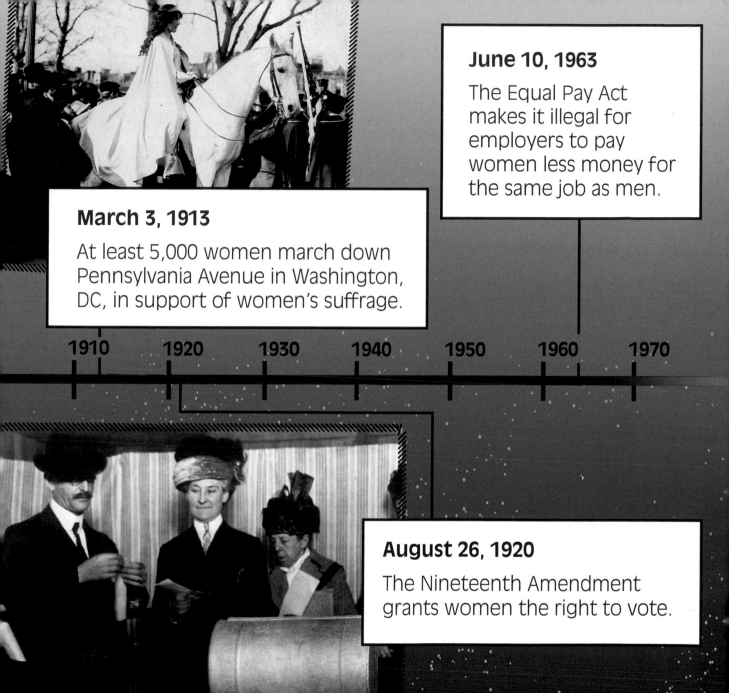

June 10, 1963

The Equal Pay Act makes it illegal for employers to pay women less money for the same job as men.

March 3, 1913

At least 5,000 women march down Pennsylvania Avenue in Washington, DC, in support of women's suffrage.

1910 1920 1930 1940 1950 1960 1970

August 26, 1920

The Nineteenth Amendment grants women the right to vote.

13

The women's suffrage movement had many leaders. Elizabeth Cady Stanton and Susan B. Anthony formed the National Woman Suffrage Association in 1869. The same year, Lucy Stone and her husband, Henry Blackwell, formed the American Woman Suffrage Association. It pushed for voting rights at state and local levels, while Anthony and Stanton's group focused on national elections.

Elizabeth Cady Stanton was a talented writer. She is believed to have been the main writer of the Declaration of Sentiments from the convention in Seneca Falls.

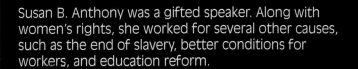

In 1890, the groups united to form the National American Woman Suffrage Association, or NAWSA. Carrie Chapman Catt joined the NAWSA the year it was founded. At that point, Wyoming was the only state in which women had **full suffrage**. Catt's leadership helped them win voting rights in Colorado in 1894.

By 1896, women had won full suffrage, or the right to vote in all elections, in Wyoming, Colorado, Utah, and Idaho. In 1909, Carrie Chapman Catt formed the Woman Suffrage Party. Their goal was to gain suffrage state by state. In 1911, women won voting rights in California, followed by Kansas and Oregon in 1912.

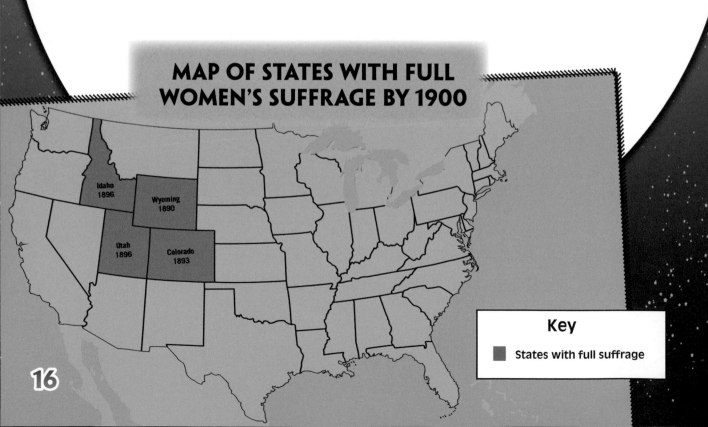

MAP OF STATES WITH FULL WOMEN'S SUFFRAGE BY 1900

Idaho
1896

Wyoming
1890

Utah
1896

Colorado
1893

Key

States with full suffrage

The US Congress got its first female member when the people of Montana elected Jeannette Rankin to the US House of Representatives in 1916.

By 1917, 13 states, most of them in the western part of the United States, had full suffrage. In many other states, women had gained **limited suffrage**, or the right to vote in only some elections. Some states, such as Texas, continued to refuse women any voting rights at all.

On March 3, 1913, more than 5,000 suffragists, or people who worked for women's suffrage, paraded down Pennsylvania Avenue in Washington, DC. Alice Paul, who planned the parade, hoped to gain the attention of President Woodrow Wilson. She also wanted to convince **Congress** to pass an amendment, or change to the Constitution. It would give women in every state full suffrage.

Carrie Chapman Catt continued to work state by state with the NAWSA, putting pressure on members of Congress to pass the amendment. It took several votes, but the Nineteenth Amendment was finally adopted on August 26, 1920. Women had won the right to vote!

These women cast their votes in San Francisco, California, soon after the passage of the Nineteenth Amendment.

Suffrage was important. It allowed women to elect leaders who supported their needs. By 1920, women had many of the rights listed in the Declaration of Sentiments. They could own land, have jobs, and go to college.

The National Women's Conference took place in Houston, Texas, in November 1977. At it, people discussed how to promote equality between men and women.

Today, women do many jobs that were once open only to men.

Though women had won many rights, they did not always receive equal treatment. In the 1960s and 1970s, Gloria Steinem, Betty Friedan, and other women in the **feminist** movement led the fight for women's rights. Their efforts saw the Equal Pay Act passed in 1963. It said that women and men must receive equal pay for the same jobs. Today women are lawyers, doctors, government leaders, and more.

From Hillary Clinton to Oprah Winfrey, today's women are more powerful than ever. In spite of this, women continue to make less money than men do. Of the millions of Americans who live in **poverty**, more than half are women.

Today, groups like the Feminist Majority Foundation and the National Organization for Women continue the fight for women's rights. They remind the world that, as the Declaration of Sentiments stated, "all men and women are created equal."

All Americans can be grateful to the brave women who fought the long battle for women's suffrage.

GLOSSARY

abolishing (uh-BAH-lish-ing) Doing away with.

amendment (uh-MEND-ment) An addition or a change to the Constitution.

American Revolution (uh-MER-uh-ken reh-vuh-LOO-shun) Battles that soldiers from the colonies fought against Britain for freedom, from 1775 to 1783.

condition (kun-DIH-shun) The way people or things are or the shape they are in.

Congress (KON-gres) The part of the US government that makes laws.

convention (kun-VEN-shun) A meeting for some special purpose.

Declaration of Independence (deh-kluh-RAY-shun UV in-duh-PEN-dints) An official announcement adopted on July 4, 1776, in which American colonists stated they were free of British rule.

feminist (FEH-mih-nist) Believing in the social equality of men and women.

full suffrage (FUL SUH-frij) The right to vote in all elections.

limited suffrage (LIH-met-ed SUH-frij) The right to vote in only some elections.

poverty (PAH-ver-tee) The state of being poor.

suffrage (SUH-frij) The right of voting.

INDEX

WEBSITES

Due to the changing nature of Internet links, PowerKids Press has developed an online list of websites related to the subject of this book. This site is updated regularly. Please use this link to access the list:
www.powerkidslinks.com/lcf/suff/